Dream Journal

Dream Journal

By Linda A. Bell
Bell Creative Studio
Las Vegas, NV 89141
(702) 518-0552

iHeart Journals
BellCreativeStudio.com

Email: Linda@BellCreativeStudio.com

© 2015 Linda A. Bell - All Rights Reserved

No part of this book may be reproduced or transmitted in any form or by any means, electronic or mechanical, including photocopying, recording or by any information storage and retrieval system without written permission from the author.

Self-Help / Journaling: use a dream journal to master the art of dreaming / Linda A. Bell -1st. ed.

ISBN-13: 978-1518688782
ISBN-10: 1518688780

Printed in the United States of America

To see the full line of iHeart Journals and learn more about author and artist, Linda A. Bell, please visit BellCreativeStudio.com

DISCLAIMER: This journal is for entertainment purposes only; it is intended to inspire creativity. The author shall have neither liability nor responsibility to any person or entity with respect to any loss or damage caused or alleged to be caused directly or indirectly by the information contained in this book.

"How to Use a Dream Journal to Master the Art of Dreaming"

by Linda A. Bell

Imagine how exciting it would be if you could ask your higher-self, the universe, and your angels for guidance, and receive the answers in your dreams.

Most people simply sleep through about a third of their life, the daily eight hour block of time in which we unplug ourselves from our conscious world to allow our brains to backup all of the data we've collected over the past sixteen hours, repair damaged cells, and rebuild our energy supply. There are those, however, who have learned how to use this "down time" to solve problems and receive clarity on their relationships, business ventures, creative projects, and personal development.

They have discovered the art of dreaming!

Like any form of art that is worth mastering, it takes practice and patience to find a technique that works best for you. Once you do, the results can be richly rewarding, profoundly insightful, brilliantly inspirational, and positively magical!

Let's get started!

Take a deep, cleansing breath. Declare that you would like to have meaningful dreams that will serve your highest good. Now open your journal and jot down a question, or an idea that you would like to flush out. This will set the wheels of intention into motion, and facilitate receiving answers.

When you go into the REM stage of sleep, your cerebral cortex, the area of your brain that is responsible for thinking, learning, and organizing your thoughts becomes activated. During this time, your unconscious mind is very receptive to learning new tasks. It can be conditioned to analyze your questions and deliver answers via dreams that are relevant and beneficial. (Putting pen to paper just before falling asleep stimulates the Reticular Activating System in your brain, and alerts it to give this question priority.) These answers come from the part of you that is connected to spirit and loves you unconditionally; the part of you that is without judgment, and helps you choose which paths to take in life.

Place your journal and a pen/pencil near your bed, where you can easily reach for it in the morning. The moment you wake up, ideally, before you step out of bed, write down everything you can remember about your dreams. Do not filter your thoughts or try to second-guess what it means. And do not be concerned about your punctuation or grammar.

Relax. Let the words flow onto the paper.

Write in the present tense. *I am walking through the woods. I see a beautiful waterfall…*

This will anchor you to your dreams, and make them more vivid.

Make little sketches; even stick figure drawings can help you recall details later, when your memories begin to fade.

As you are journaling, use your sensory and extrasensory perceptions to describe what you are seeing, hearing, smelling, tasting, touching, and feeling. Do you see any colors? Who are you with? Do you notice anything unusual or odd about your surroundings? Did you wake up with a number or a phrase stuck in your head, as if someone had just whispered it to you?

Our dreams will often create more questions than answers. That's good! Write them down. It's all part of the process. Over time, you will learn how to read between the lines of what you have written, and intuitively interpret the underlying messages. Sometimes, it can take several days or even weeks for the meaning of your dreams to become evident. Be sure to notate these discoveries!

Dream Signs

Dream signs are impressionistic, and can rarely be taken literally. Refer back to the question that you asked to see how these signs are being used in the sentence, so to speak, to convey the answer.

To wrap your head around this concept, it may be helpful to visualize yourself playing a game of charades with a cast of dream characters who are holding up props to see which ones will get an "aha!" response out of you.

Some of your dream signs may include:

- **Animals, Insects**
- **Buildings**
- **Colors**
- **Elements: fire, air, water, wind, sky/heaven**
- **Flowers, grass, gardens, trees**
- **Numbers, words, phrases**
- **Objects of all kinds**
- **People**
- **Places**

Close your eyes and take a closer look at every dream sign that you can recall. Document them to the best of your ability. This teaches your unconscious and conscious mind how to work together to send you messages that are clear and concise. As your dream sign vocabulary increases, so will your knack for deciphering the messages you receive.

Types of Dreams

The intensity of your dreams will increase as your unconscious mind becomes more self-aware. You will likely notice an increase in the following types of dreams:

- **Cathartic Dreams:** these provide answers that help you release anger, frustration, and fears; they restore peace and confidence
- **Inspirational Dreams:** ideas come to you that can be incorporated into your business plans, art, music compositions, inventions, etc.
- **Lucid Dreams:** you are consciously aware of the fact that you are in a dream; you are able to think about what you are doing, and can control your actions
- **Multi-Level (aka False-Awakening) Dreams:** in this dream, you feel like you've just woken up from another dream and can often recall details about it
- **Premonition Dreams:** a dream about something that is going to happen in the future
- **Psychic Dreams:** very specific, factual information comes to you in a dream about things, people, or situations that you could not possibly know about otherwise
- **Recurring Dreams:** the same dream, over and over
- **Telepathic Dreams:** you receive a message from someone while you are asleep
- **Wishful Dreams:** in these dreams, your wishes are fulfilled

One of the most remarkable things about Lucid Dreaming is that you can actually learn how to do it well. Advanced lucid dream practitioners can speak directly to their past and future selves, communicate with other dream characters, seek out spirit guides, find solutions to problems, receive creative ideas, fly through the air with precision, conquer nightmares, and travel to anywhere their heart desires, all while their body is resting.

Imagine the possibilities…

Have fun journaling!

In my dreams...

Date: / /

Date: /   /

Date: /   /

Date: /   /

Date: / /

Date: /   /

Date: /   /

Date: /   /

Date: / /

Date: /   /

Date: / /

Date: / /

Date: / /

Date: /   /

Date: / /

Date: / /

Date: /   /

Date: /   /

Date: / /

Date: / /

Date: /   /

Date: / /

Date: / /

Date: / /

Date: / /

Date: / /

Date: /   /

Date: / /

Date: / /

Date: / /

Date: / /

Date: /   /

Date: /   /

Date: /   /

Date: / /

Date: /   /

Date: /   /

Date: / /

Date: /   /

Date: / /

Date: /   /

Date: / /

Date: / /

Date: /   /

Date: / /

Date: / /

Date: /   /

Date: /   /

Date: /   /

Date: /   /

Date: / /

Date: / /

Date: / /

Date: / /

Date: /   /

Date: / /

Date: /   /

Date: /   /

Date: / /

Date: / /

Date: / /

Date: / /

Date: / /

Date: /   /

Date: / /

Date: /   /

Date: / /

Date: / /

Date: /   /

Printed in Great Britain
by Amazon